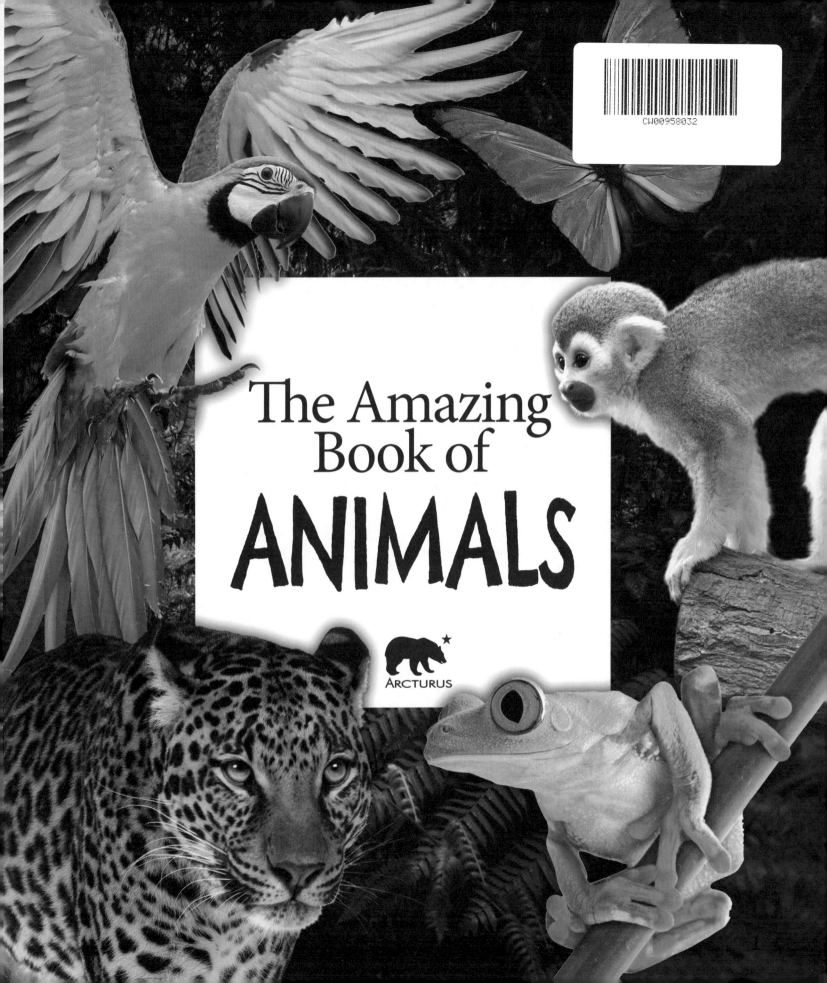

The Amazing Book of ANIMALS

ARCTURUS

Picture Credits:
Key: b–bottom, t–top, c–center, l–left, r–right

Alamy: 4–5 (Ian Cruickshank), 9cr (Fernando Quevedo de Oliveira), 22/23 (Suzi Eszterhas/Minden Pictures), 30–31 (Alejandro Díaz Díez/age fotostock), 46–47 (Richard Becker); **FLPA:** cover main (Chris Brunskill), cover tc (Martin Willis/Minden Pictures), cover tcr (Michael & Patricia Fogden/Minden Pictures), 6–7 (Frans Lanting), 12–13 (Christopher Swan/Biosphoto), 20cl (Juergen & Christine Sohns/Minden Pictures), 27t (Alan Murphy/Minden Pictures), 29cr (Konrad Wothe), 32cl (Reinhard Dirscherl), 33cr (Daniel Heuclin/Biosphoto), 34–35 (Artur Cupak/Imagebroker), 34bl (Paul van Hoof/Minden Pictures), 36b (Thomas Marent/Minden Pictures), 38b (Norbert Probst/Imagebroker), 44–45 (Peter Schwarz, BIA/Minden Pictures), 44bl (Piotr Naskrecki/Minden Pictures), 45cr (Michel Gunther/Biosphoto) ; **Shutterstock:** cover tl (Aleksey Stemmer), cover tcl (Tyler Fox), cover tr (worldswildlifewonders), 1 (Nuamfolio), 4cl (Puwadol Jaturawutthichai), 4br (Alen thien), 5tr (Giedrilius), 5cl (David Bokuchava), 5br (Dennis van de Water), 6–7 (LMIMAGES), 6bl (belizar), 7tl (Medvedeva Oxana), 7br (Luna Photogood), 8bl (Victor Lapaev), 9br (Spreadthesign), 10–11 (Warren Metcalf), 10bl (Michal Ninger), 11cr (davemhuntphotography), 11br (SaveJungle), 16–17 (Sergey Uryadnikov), 16cl (sirtravelalot), 17tr (elmm), 17br (Photo by Lola), 12cl (Michael Smith/ITWP), 12br (Kurilin Gennadiy Nikolaevich), 13b (Tory Kallman), 18–19 (Nuamfolio), 18tr (Utopia_88), 19tr (Maquiladora), 19cr (Nivlac921), 20br (Noahsu), 21br (Yana Kazuar), 22c (Andril Slonchak), 22br (Creative Mood), 23cr (Jason Benz Bennee), 24–25 (Fotos593), 24cl (robert mcgillivray), 24cr (chaika), 25br (YK), 26–27 (MZPHOTO.CZ), 26cl (Jan_Broz), 26br (Ovan Feoktistov), 28–29 (laurent caputoGustavo Frazao), 28c (Gustavo Frazao), 28br (Panda Vector), 30cr (Fabio Maffei), 30br (Savo Ilic), 31br (Maquiladora), 32–33 (reptiles4all), 32br (Park Ji Sun), 35cr (Abhindia), 35br (RinArte), 36–37 (Michael Fitzsimmons), 36tr (Sergey Uryadnikov), 37tr (SaveJungle), 38–39 (Damsea), 38c (Aries Sutanto), 39br (Juncat), 40–41 (wildestanimal), 40cl (Grant M Henderson), 41tr (Adisom Chaikit), 41br (Voinau Pavel), 42–43 (Florian Teodor), 42tr (Gmarosso), 42br (Vectorworks_Enterprise), 43cr (Jarun Tedjaem), 45br (Alastair Wallace), 46c (Sally Wallis), 46br (foodonwhite), 47br (Kostiantyn Kravchenko).

ARCTURUS

This edition published in 2019 by Arcturus Publishing Limited
26/27 Bickels Yard, 151–153 Bermondsey Street,
London SE1 3HA

Authors: Michael Leach and Meriel Lland
Editors: Clare Hibbert and Samantha Hilton
Designers: Amy McSimpson and Trudi Webb

ISBN: 978-1-78950-834-5
CH007560NT
Supplier 29, Date 0719, Print run 9205

Printed in China

The Amazing Book of ANIMALS

CONTENTS

Introduction

Rhinoceros hornbills are birds that live in Southeast Asian rain forests. Birds are warm-blooded animals with backbones. They have wings and most can fly.

An animal is a living organism made up of cells. It feeds, senses and responds to its surroundings, moves, and reproduces. Scientists have identified nearly nine million species of living animals, but there are many more to be found.

Life Appears

Single-celled life forms appeared around four billion years ago. Sponges—the first animals—appeared a billion years ago. Over time, more complicated animals evolved and some also became extinct. Dinosaurs were the dominant land animals for 165 million years before they died out 65 million years ago.

Fossilized skull of the dinosaur, *Tyrannosaurus rex*

Leaf beetle, an insect

Classifying Life

Scientists organize living things into groups with shared characteristics. The two main kinds of animal are ones with backbones (vertebrates) and ones without (invertebrates). Arthropods make up the biggest invertebrate group. They have segmented bodies and jointed limbs. Insects, spiders, and crabs are all arthropods.

Warm- and Cold-Blooded

Most animals are ectothermic, or "cold-blooded." Their body temperature is controlled by their environment. Mammals and birds are endothermic, or "warm-blooded." Their bodies can generate their own heat, so they can survive in much colder habitats.

Musk ox, a mammal

Langurs in a city

Fragile Earth

We are lucky to share our world with an extraordinary richness of animals. It is important to protect our wildlife. When humans pollute or damage the environment, we harm both animals and people. The future is in our hands.

Animal Habitats

The place where an animal lives is called its habitat. Animals have evolved to inhabit just about every environment on Earth, from tropical rain forests and coral reefs to deserts, mountain tops, and ice floes. They even survive in cities.

Giant leaf–tailed gecko, vulnerable because of habitat loss

5

Carnivores

Mammals are warm-blooded, breathe air, and have a backbone. They give birth to live young, which they feed with mother's milk. Carnivores are mammals that eat meat. Nearly 300 mammal species are true carnivores. They live all over the globe and in all habitats.

Carnivore Features

Carnivorous mammals are built to spot, chase, and kill prey. They have forward-facing eyes that judge distance and long legs for speed. Their large brains help them to hunt strategically. Some carnivores live solitary lives, but others live in packs or groups and hunt as a team.

Carnivores have specialized teeth: long, pointed canines at the front of the mouth for killing and sharp-edged carnassials at the back for slicing through meat.

Living Fast

Meat is rich in energy, so carnivores don't need to feed often. When they do hunt, it helps to be in peak condition. Any illness or slight injury slows them. Predators' lives are dangerous and can be short. More predators die of starvation than old age.

A leopard can eat 4 kg (9 lb) of meat at a time. It only needs to hunt twice a week, and can spend the rest of the time resting.

The hyena's crushing bite lets it reach the rich marrow inside bones. Around half of its diet is carrion.

SPOTTED HYENA

CROCUTA CROCUTA

Habitat: Woodlands, grasslands, scrub; sub-Saharan Africa
Length: Male 1.3 m (4.3 ft); female 1.4 m (4.6 ft)
Weight: Male 55 kg (121 lb); female 60 kg (132 lb)
Diet: Mammals
Lifespan: Up to 20 years
Wild population: 40,000; Least Concern

Cats

Cats are carnivores with soft fur, a short snout, and sharp claws. The first cats appeared around 30 million years ago. Today wild cats live everywhere except Australia and the Antarctic. There are 41 wild cat species. Four— the lion, tiger, jaguar, and leopard— are in their own family: the big cats.

Forward–facing eyes let this Bengal tiger judge distance accurately. Most cats are nocturnal hunters and see well in the dark.

Getting a Grip

Cats use their sharp claws to grab prey. In most species the claws retract into the paw when they are not being used. However, the cheetah's claws are always out. They grip the ground and stop the cat slipping when it runs.

The cheetah is the world's fastest mammal. In short bursts it can sprint at 105 km/h (65 mph).

Hearing is a tiger's most important sense. The cat can swivel each ear independently to pick up faraway sounds from all directions.

Long, sensitive whiskers can detect small air movements. This is useful for finding prey at night.

Stripes camouflage tigers in forests and grasslands. Tigers spend an hour every day licking their fur. This removes loose hairs and keeps the coat clean and warm.

The large, sharp canine teeth kill prey. Behind these, the carnassial teeth are used for cutting through flesh.

Family Life

Lions are the only cats that hunt and live in groups. All other species are loners that come together only to breed. Most cats live in forests or grasslands, but some have adapted to other environments. Sand cats live in deserts, hunting birds and lizards and surviving on very little water.

Lions live in family groups called prides. A typical pride includes related lionesses, their cubs, and a couple of adult males.

BENGAL TIGER

PANTHERA TIGRIS
"CAT TIGER"

Habitat: Forests, swamps, grasslands; S Asia
Length: Male 3 m (9.8 ft); female 2.6 m (8.5 ft)
Weight: Male 250 kg (551 lb);
  female 160 kg (353 lb)
Diet: Mammals—e.g. deer, wild pigs
Lifespan: Up to 18 years
Wild population: 2,000–2,500;
Endangered

Wolves

The largest members of the dog family, timber wolves were once the most widely distributed predator on Earth. Today they live only in remote areas of North America and Eurasia, far from humans, but their population is stable. However, the red wolf from the eastern United States and the Ethiopian wolf are both endangered.

Falling Numbers

For centuries, humans hunted wolves because they feared attacks on themselves and their livestock. They also cleared wolves' forest habitats for farmland. Today the timber wolf is extinct in much of Western Europe, Mexico, and the United States.

Flattened ears give this wolf's body a streamlined shape when it runs. In an encounter with another wolf, flattened ears would be a sign of submission.

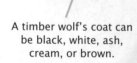
A timber wolf's coat can be black, white, ash, cream, or brown.

Wolves can smell prey up to 1.6 km (1 mile) away. The nose also tells them whether another wolf is a friend or rival, and whether it has just eaten.

The thick coat is waterproof and warm, thanks to a dense undercoat. Wolves survive at temperatures down to −40°C (−40°F).

Tails are used for balance and communication. Dominant wolves hold their tail high. Low-ranking animals curl their tail between their legs.

Long legs and stamina mean a wolf can cover 96 km (60 miles) in just six hours. During a chase it can reach 56 km/h (35 mph).

Wolves mark territory by howling and leaving strong-smelling droppings.

Family Affair

A pack's territory can range from just 30 sq km (11.6 sq miles) to as much as 2,000 sq km (770 sq miles). A typical pack contains about a dozen animals. Only the dominant male and female breed. The other pack members work together to protect the cubs.

TIMBER WOLF

CANIS LUPUS "WOLF DOG"

Habitat: Forests, tundra, mountains, grasslands; N America, Asia, Europe
Length: 3 m (9.8 ft)
Weight: Male 45 kg (99 lb); female 38.5 kg (85 lb)
Diet: Mammals—e.g. deer, buffalo
Lifespan: Up to 12 years
Wild population: Unknown; Least Concern

Whales and Dolphins

A pod of short-beaked common dolphins work together to attack a baitball of blue jack mackerel.

Dolphins and whales are cetaceans—highly intelligent mammals that mate, feed, and give birth in all the world's oceans. Cetaceans are split into two groups: baleen whales, which eat invertebrates, and toothed whales, such as dolphins, which take much bigger prey.

Filter-Feeders

Blue whales, humpbacks, and other baleen whales are filter-feeders. These huge animals have sieve-like plates inside their mouths to filter plankton, krill, or other foods from the water.

This is a baby humpback whale. Baby whales drink the equivalent of one-and-a-third full bathtubs of mother's milk a day!

COMMON DOLPHIN

DELPHINUS DELPHIS
"DOLPHIN DOLPHIN"

Habitat: Atlantic, Pacific, Indian Ocean, Mediterranean Sea
Length: Male 2.2 m (7.2 ft);
   female 2.1 m (6.9 ft)
Weight: Male 120 kg (265 lb);
   female 105 kg (231 lb)
Diet: Fish, squid, octopus
Lifespan: Around 20 years
Wild population: Unknown: Least Concern

Dolphins travel in pods of up to 1,000. They live mainly in warm waters, hunting fish and squid.

The dolphins herded the fish into a ball shape. It is easy to pick off individuals from the edge of the ball.

Finding Food

Dolphins and other toothed whales use echolocation to navigate and find prey. They produce clicks that travel through the water and then bounce back to them off objects. Cetaceans also use noises to communicate with each other. Humpbacks are known for their long, complex songs.

The orca is the largest species of dolphin. It mostly hunts seals, but also eats squid, sea birds, fish, and even turtles.

Omnivores and Herbivores

Some mammals eat both meat and plants. These are the omnivores, adaptable species that survive on a wide variety of food. Herbivores are specialists that eat only vegetation—leaves, grass, flowers, bark, and other plant parts.

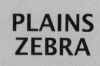

PLAINS ZEBRA

EQUUS QUAGGA

Habitat: Forests, grasslands, scrub; E & S Africa
Length: Male 2.3 m (7.5 ft);
 female 2 m (6.6 ft)
Weight: Male 300 kg (661 lb);
 female 250 kg (551 lb)
Diet: Grass, low-growing plants
Lifespan: Up to 25 years
Wild population: 750,000; Near Threatened

Varied Diet

Omnivores have more choice than specialists. They can eat foods that are in season and change their diet if a particular food source dries up.

Zebra and wildebeest are herbivores. Grazers have sharp front teeth called incisors to snip off plants, and big, flat back teeth called molars for chewing.

A badger feasts on fruit when it is in season, eats worms when it's raining, and catches small mammals when it can.

Digestive Challenges

Plants are hard to digest. Some animals, such as rabbits, get around this by eating their droppings. As the food passes through the body a second time, they absorb any remaining goodness. Other animals simply take a long time to process their food.

Food passes through the human body in about 30 hours, but in a sloth this can take up to three weeks!

15

Bears

There are eight species of bear. They live in Asia, Europe, and the Americas. Most are omnivores that feed on plants and insects and live in forest habitats. They only eat meat if they find carrion or a slow-moving, weak animal. Polar bears are the exception. These speedy hunters are carnivores.

The Bear's Year

Polar bears are active all year round, but other bears in the far north—grizzlies and black bears—hibernate in winter. In warmer places, there is plenty of food all year. Species such as Indian sloth bears don't need a winter sleep.

Underneath the dense, waterproof fur is a thick layer of fatty blubber to protect the polar bear from the cold.

When salmon swim upriver to breed in late summer, grizzlies have a fishy feast! It helps them put on weight ready for hibernation.

Bears are usually loners, but mothers look after their cubs for two years or more. The cubs grow quickly because their mother's milk is about one-third fat.

POLAR BEAR

URSUS MARITIMUS
"SEA BEAR"

Habitat: Tundra, ice floes, oceans; Arctic
Length: Male 2.8 m (9.2 ft);
    female 2.4 m (7.2 ft)
Weight: Male 600 kg (1,323 lb);
    female 260 kg (573 lb)
Diet: Seals, carrion, fish
Lifespan: Up to 25 years
Wild population: 30,000; Vulnerable

All bears have amazingly sensitive noses. They can smell food up to 50 km (30 miles) away.

Picky Pandas

Most bears eat many kinds of food, but pandas are choosy. Ninety-nine percent of their diet is bamboo. Pandas live in the mountains of China. They are threatened by habitat loss and only around 1,500 are left in the wild.

The bear's pale, creamy coat helps to camouflage it against the snow.

Most mammals are digitigrade—they walk on their toes. Bears (and humans) are plantigrade—they stand on the soles of their feet.

Pandas spend most of their waking hours eating. They eat about 600 bamboo stems a day.

17

Elephants

Elephants evolved 50 million years ago. The two kinds alive today are African and Asian elephants. They live in family groups of up to 12 females and their calves, led by an older female called the matriarch. Adult male elephants live alone or in male-only herds.

African or Asian?

The African elephant is the world's largest land animal. One male weighed 11,000 kg (24,000 lb). Asian elephants are smaller and have smaller ears. Their backs are flat or humped; the African elephant's back has a dip in the middle.

Elephant babies take longer to develop inside their mother than any other land mammal. The mother elephant is pregnant for 22 months.

The front teeth, or tusks, dig up roots and strip bark from trees. Inside the mouth, four huge molars grind up plant food.

The ears are used as fans to cool the elephant on hot days. Each elephant can be identified by the shape and size of its ears.

ASIAN ELEPHANT

ELEPHAS MAXIMUS
"LARGEST OX"

Habitat: Forests, scrub; S Asia
Length: Male 3 m (9.8 ft);
  female 2.7 m (8.9 ft)
Weight: Male 4,500 kg (9,921 lb);
  female 2,750 kg (6,063 lb)
Diet: Leaves, twigs, bark
Lifespan: Up to 60 years
Wild population: 40,000; Endangered

Trunk Talk

The elephant's trunk is an extension of its nose and top lip. It is incredibly sensitive and versatile. It can carry food and water into the mouth, squirt water, or spray dust. It is also used to touch and stroke.

Elephants suck up dust and then blow it over their back and shoulders. It acts as a sunscreen and keeps away insects.

The tail is 1.3 m (4 ft) long and tipped with long, thick hair. It can be flicked like a fly swat to drive away insects.

The trunk is so complicated that it takes a calf a year to master using it! It can grasp, suck, touch, and smell.

Apes

The orangutan is the only ape that lives alone instead of in groups. However, a young orangutan stays with its mother for the first eight years of life.

Apes are primates that do not have tails. There are two groups. The great apes are humans, Central Africa's chimpanzees and gorillas, and the orangutan of Borneo and Sumatra. The lesser apes are the 18 gibbon species, which are smaller than their great ape cousins.

Intelligent Beasts

The great apes are large, intelligent animals. They have very advanced brains, great memories, and are good at solving problems. Chimpanzees are the most frequent tool users. They use sticks as "fishing rods" to collect termites from termite mounds. They also shape sticks into "spears" for hunting small primates. Chimps are the only apes that regularly eat meat. The protein helps to fuel their big brains.

A chimpanzee slurps up termites from its "fishing" stick. It even frays the end of the stick so it will pick up more insects.

Under Threat

All the non-human great apes are endangered, and gorillas and orangutans are critically endangered. They have been affected by habitat destruction, hunting, and disease, and have also been removed from the wild for the illegal pet trade.

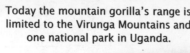

Today the mountain gorilla's range is limited to the Virunga Mountains and one national park in Uganda.

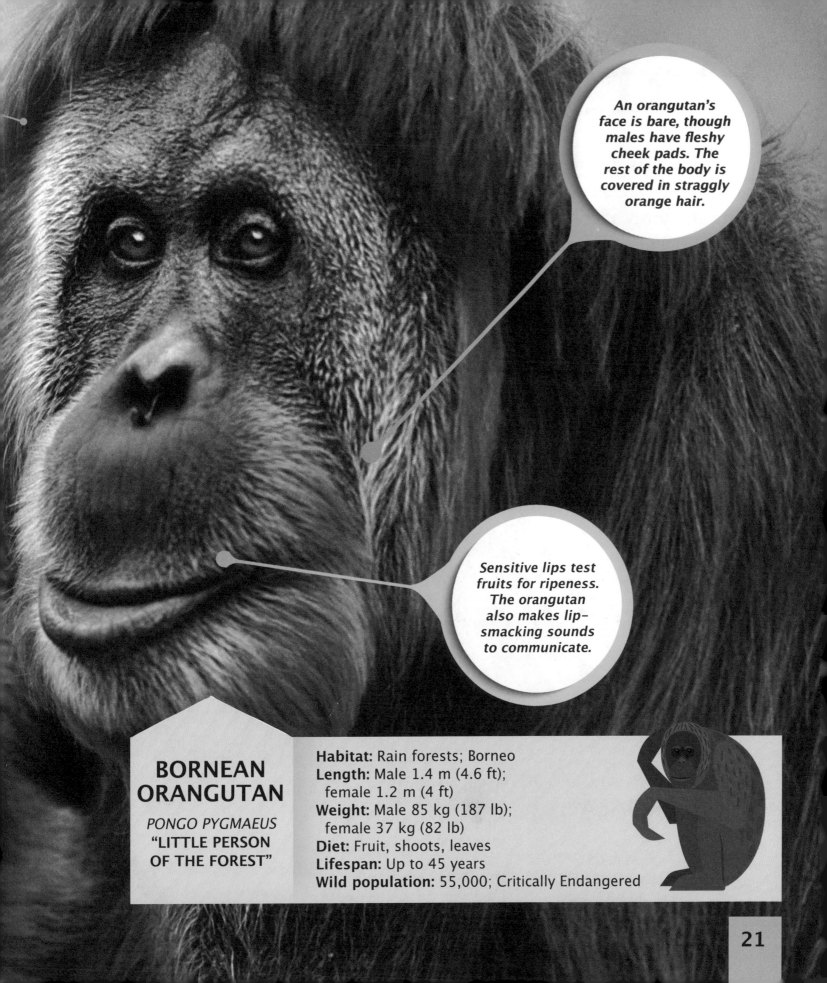

An orangutan's face is bare, though males have fleshy cheek pads. The rest of the body is covered in straggly orange hair.

Sensitive lips test fruits for ripeness. The orangutan also makes lip-smacking sounds to communicate.

BORNEAN ORANGUTAN

PONGO PYGMAEUS
"LITTLE PERSON OF THE FOREST"

Habitat: Rain forests; Borneo
Length: Male 1.4 m (4.6 ft); female 1.2 m (4 ft)
Weight: Male 85 kg (187 lb); female 37 kg (82 lb)
Diet: Fruit, shoots, leaves
Lifespan: Up to 45 years
Wild population: 55,000; Critically Endangered

Marsupials

Kangaroos, koalas, and their relatives are marsupials, or pouched mammals. Most mammal babies develop inside their mother's body, and many can walk or even run shortly after birth. Marsupial babies are born tiny, underdeveloped, and helpless. They crawl into their mother's pouch to carry on growing there.

Australian Life

There are a few marsupial species, such as the opossums, in North and South America. However, most live in Australia and New Guinea. They include kangaroos, koalas, wombats, wallabies, quokkas, and Tasmanian devils. Pouched mammals were the only kind of mammal in Australia until early settlers brought non-native dogs, mice, and rabbits.

The large nose sniffs out fresh eucalyptus leaves and scent markings left by other koalas.

The red kangaroo is the largest marsupial. This young male will grow almost as tall as a human, be able to leap 9 m (29.5 ft), and run at 70 km/h (44 mph).

The mother's pouch holds the baby koala, which is called a joey.

KOALA

PHASCOLARCTOS CINEREUS

"ASHY POUCHED BEAR"

Habitat: Forests, scrub; E Australia
Length: Male 75 cm (30 in); female 70 cm (28 in)
Weight: Male 9 kg (19.8 lb); female 7 kg (15.4 lb)
Diet: Eucalyptus leaves
Lifespan: Up to 20 years
Wild population: 75,000; Vulnerable

All Sorts of Diet

Kangaroos and wallabies eat any grass or leaves, while koalas feed mainly on eucalyptus. Insect-eating marsupials, such as bilbies, bandicoots, and numbats, have pointed snouts for winkling minibeasts out of bark or soil. The Tasmanian devil is the largest carnivorous marsupial.

The Tasmanian devil is the size of a small dog but it can take prey as large as a medium kangaroo.

Extremely thick, waterproof fur protects the koala against hot and cold temperatures.

Birds

Birds are warm-blooded animals with feathers, whose front limbs have evolved into wings. They have toothless, beaked jaws and their young hatch from eggs. There are nearly 11,000 species of bird. They communicate with each other using songs and calls, and some are amazing mimics.

High Flyers

Some birds, such as penguins, have lost the power of flight but many fly extraordinary distances. Some birds are so well adapted to flight that they rarely land. The wandering albatross can stay on the wing for distances up to 16,090 km (10,000 miles).

The wandering albatross has the widest wingspan of any bird—up to 3.5 m (11.5 ft) across.

HOATZIN

OPISTHOCOMUS HOAZIN

"PHEASANT WITH LONG HAIR BEHIND"

Habitat: Swamps, forests; S America
Length: 65 cm (25.6 in)
Wingspan: 50 cm (20 in)
Weight: 800 g (1.8 lb)
Diet: Leaves, fruit, flowers
Lifespan: Up to 10 years
Wild population: Unknown; Least concern

The hoatzin communicates with loud, wheezy groans, clucks, growls, and hisses.

Eggs and Nests

Birds reproduce by laying hard-shelled eggs that need to be incubated (kept at a warm, steady temperature). Most birds sit on their eggs and use their own body heat to keep them warm. When the eggs hatch, most chicks are helpless. They rely on their parents to bring them food.

Birds evolved from theropods, carnivorous dinosaurs that walked on two legs. Their feathers developed from scales.

Blackbird chicks open their beaks for food from their father. Only the female blackbird incubates the eggs, but both parents feed the chicks.

Owls

Owls are raptors, or hunting birds, found almost everywhere except the Antarctic. There are around 200 species, ranging from the tiny, insect-eating elf owl to the Eurasian eagle owl that takes prey as large as deer. Owls are solitary birds and most of them are active only at night.

The enormous eyes let in as much light as possible when the owl is hunting at night. They are also very sensitive to movement.

Super Senses

Owls have huge, forward-facing eyes and can swivel their head 270 degrees to gain good all-round vision. Owls also have excellent hearing. They fly so silently that they can hear the faint rustlings of small mammals down on the ground.

Strong feet with sharp talons can catch and kill small animals. The bottom of each foot has rough, knobbly skin that gives extra grip on struggling prey.

The long-eared owl is named for the feathered tufts on its head, but these are not actually ears. They are just there to make the owl look bigger.

BARN OWL

TYTO ALBA
"WHITE OWL"

Habitat: Grasslands, farmland, scrub; Almost worldwide
Length: 37 cm (1.2 ft)
Wingspan: Male 90 cm (3 ft); female 105 cm (3.4 ft)
Weight: Male 470 g (1 lb); female 570 g (1.3 lb)
Diet: Small mammals, amphibians, lizards, insects
Lifespan: Up to 5 years
Wild population: Unknown; Least Concern

No Place Like Home

Owls are one of the few birds that don't make their own nest. They reuse other birds' old nests or lay their eggs in a hollow tree. Some owls bring up their chicks in the rafters of a barn. Others find a rocky ledge, a hollow in the ground, or even a burrow.

Eastern screech owls use any natural or artificial cavity as a nesting site. These chicks are being raised in a nestbox.

The super-soft feathers make almost no noise in flight because fringed wing edges muffle any sound. The owl flies silently.

Hidden beneath feathers are sensitive ears that can detect a mouse moving through grass from a distance of 10 m (33 ft).

Showing Off

Some birds advertise for a mate or announce their ownership of a territory with complicated songs. Others signal with vibrant feathers and displays that rivals can easily see. Bird feathers are some of the most eye-catching objects in the animal world.

Forest Feathers

Many rain forest-dwelling birds rely on dazzling plumage to find a mate in the gloom of the jungle. From birds-of-paradise to parrots, these birds have showy feathers in a rainbow of hues. Toucans draw attention to themselves with a different feature—their large, bright bill!

The peacock's heavy train (tail) makes up more than 60 percent of its body weight. The healthiest, fittest males have the biggest, flashiest trains.

The Indian peafowl is native to forests in South Asia. Prized for the male's spectacular plumage, it has been introduced to parks and other habitats all over the world.

The toco toucan lives in South America. Its enormous orange bill is up to 23 cm (9.1 in) long—that's a third of the bird's body length.

INDIAN PEAFOWL

PAVO CRISTATUS
"CRESTED PEAFOWL"

Habitat: Forests, farmland, grassland; S Asia
Length: Male 2.1 m (6.9 ft); female 0.95 m (3.1 ft)
Wingspan: Male 1.5 m (4.9 ft); female 1.2 m (3.9 ft)
Weight: Male 5.5 kg (12.1 lb); female 3.5 kg (7.7 lb)
Diet: Insects, seeds, fruit, reptiles, small mammals
Lifespan: Up to 30 years
Wild population: Unknown; Least Concern

Each tail feather ends with a striking eyespot. The bird shakes and rattles the fanned-out train for added effect.

Courtship

The male bowerbird wins the prize for the most extraordinary courtship display. First it builds an arched structure called a bower from dried grasses. Then it collects and arranges beautiful objects in front of the bower. Female birds tour several bowers before they decide on a mate.

A male satin bowerbird displays feathers, petals, shells, wrappers, and bottle tops in front of its bower—anything as long as it is blue!

The highlights on the iridescent green feathers shift from silver to blue, depending on the light.

Reptiles and Amphibians

Reptiles and amphibians are both animal groups that are vertebrates (have backbones) and cannot make their own body heat (are "cold-blooded" or ectothermic). Reptiles include lizards, alligators, crocodiles, turtles, and snakes. Amphibians include frogs, toads, and salamanders.

Water and Land

Amphibians spend their early life in water, breathing through gills, then develop lungs and live on land. Their name means "two lives." Amphibian skin is thin, but reptiles have scaly, watertight skin. Most reptiles live on land and they all use lungs to breathe air—even sea turtles. "Reptile" comes from the Latin word for "crawling."

The caecilian is a strange, worm-like amphibian. Most species live underground. They use their needle-sharp teeth to eat worms, termites, and even snakes, frogs, and lizards.

Metamorphosis

Almost all amphibians undergo a change, or metamorphosis. With its gills and fishy tail, a tadpole looks nothing like its parents. At five weeks its back legs sprout and by ten weeks, the froglet has front legs and a shorter tail. By 14 weeks, it looks like a tiny frog.

Frog larvae (young) are called tadpoles. They do not have legs yet but they have a tail that helps them to swim.

A few reptiles give birth to live young, but most lay eggs. The eggs are soft, like thick paper. This hatchling is a green iguana.

GREEN IGUANA

IGUANA IGUANA

Habitat: Forests; C & S America
Length: Male 1.8 m (5.9ft); female 1.5 m (4.9 ft)
Weight: Male 4 kg (9 lb); female 3 kg (6.6 lb)
Diet: Leaves, flowers, fruit
Lifespan: Up to 20 years
Wild population: Unknown; Least Concern

Deadly Snakes

Some snakes paralyze or kill their prey by injecting it with venom. Venomous snakes include cobras, vipers, rattlesnakes, and death adders. They are smaller than constrictors (snakes that kill by squeezing), but they can move fast. The black mamba hits 20 km/h (12 mph)!

Deadly Killers

Australia is home to some of the world's most venomous snakes: tiger snakes, taipans, and brown snakes. Other deadly species include kraits, sea kraits, and sea snakes. Sea snakes inhabit warm, tropical oceans. They breathe air but spend their lives in water.

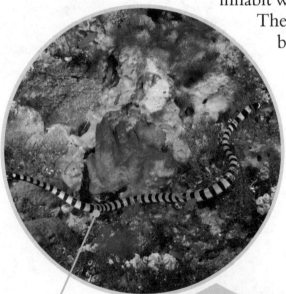

Many vipers have heat-sensing pits that detect prey's body heat. Bush vipers do not have these pits.

The banded sea krait's black and yellow stripes warn that it is extremely venomous.

BUSH VIPER

ATHERIS SQUAMIGERA

Habitat: Forests; Central Africa
Length: Male 65 cm (25.6 in); female 70 cm (27.6 in)
Weight: Male 400 g (0.9 lb); female 650 g (1.4 lb)
Diet: Birds, reptiles, rodents, amphibians
Lifespan: Up to 20 years
Wild population: Unknown; Vulnerable

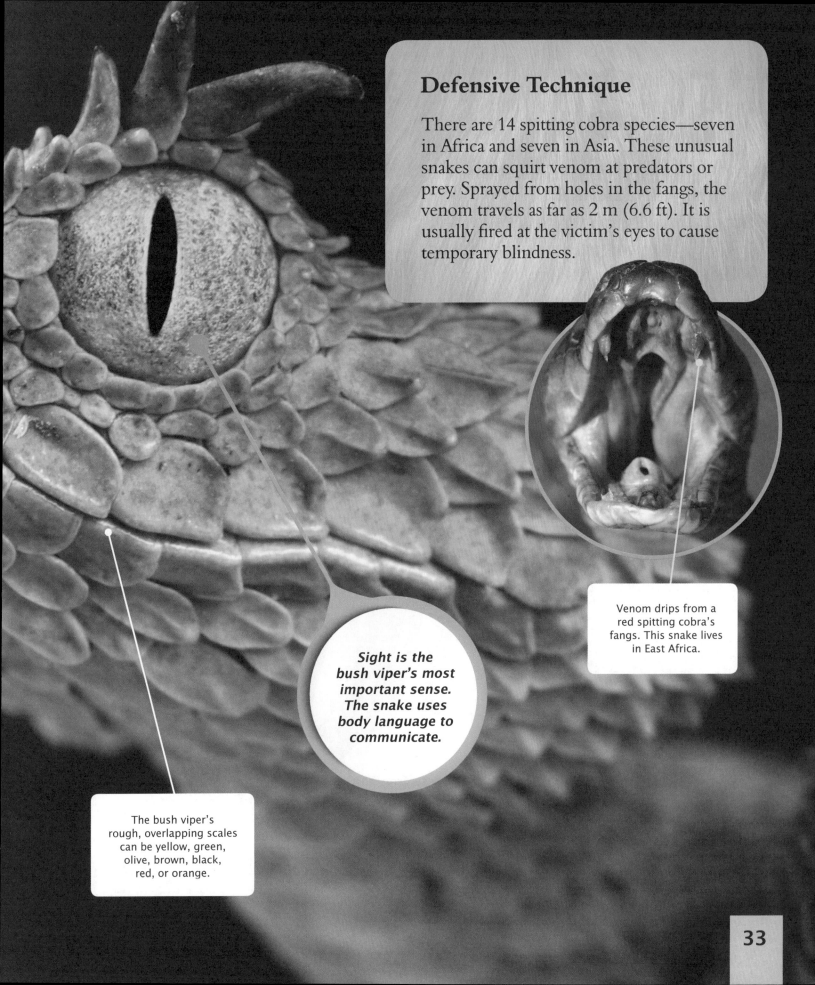

Defensive Technique

There are 14 spitting cobra species—seven in Africa and seven in Asia. These unusual snakes can squirt venom at predators or prey. Sprayed from holes in the fangs, the venom travels as far as 2 m (6.6 ft). It is usually fired at the victim's eyes to cause temporary blindness.

Sight is the bush viper's most important sense. The snake uses body language to communicate.

Venom drips from a red spitting cobra's fangs. This snake lives in East Africa.

The bush viper's rough, overlapping scales can be yellow, green, olive, brown, black, red, or orange.

Frogs

Frogs are by far the most common kind of amphibian—there are around 4,800 different species. They range in size from a tiny 7-mm (0.3-in) frog that lives on the floor of Papua New Guinea's rain forests (and holds the record for smallest vertebrate) to Africa's well-named 32-cm (12.6-in) goliath frog.

Frogs on the Move

Most frogs are strong swimmers and exceptional jumpers. Their legs have stretchy muscles that are pulled in when the frog is at rest. If an enemy approaches, the legs kick back and the muscles act as a spring to push the frog through the air.

The frog has a large, sensitive ear behind each eye. It has keen hearing.

Frogs jump horizontally rather than up into the air. Many species can leap more than 20 times their own body length.

The tree frog has sticky pads at the end of its fingers and toes for extra grip.

A frog blinks when it swallows its food. This pushes its eyes into the head, forcing the struggling insect down the frog's throat.

Skin Deep

Poison dart frogs live in Central and South American rain forests and come in eye-catching blues, reds, greens, oranges, yellows, and blacks. Their bright skin is a warning to predators that it tastes bad and contains toxic chemicals. The most poisonous, the golden poison frog, contains enough toxin to kill up to 20 people.

Bulging eyes can see about 280 degrees all around. This is useful because the frog cannot bend its neck.

Poison dart frogs are tiny. The largest species, this dyeing dart frog, is just 5 cm (2 in) long.

RED–EYED TREE FROG

AGALYCHNIS CALLIDRYAS
"BEAUTIFUL SHINING TREE NYMPH"

Habitat: Rain forests; C America
Length: Male 5 cm (2 in); female 7.5 cm (3 in)
Weight: Male 10 g (0.3 oz); female 15 g (0.5 oz)
Diet: Small insects, other invertebrates
Lifespan: Up to 5 years
Wild population: Unknown; Least Concern

Crocodiles

Crocodilians are an ancient family of reptiles that appeared during the age of the dinosaurs. As well as crocodiles, they include alligators, caimans, and the gharial. Crocodilians live in and around water worldwide in warm habitats. They are fierce predators.

Man-Eaters

Large crocodilians will eat anything. The saltwater crocodile catches monkeys, deer, kangaroos, and other land animals as well as turtles, sea snakes, and sharks. It has the strongest bite of any animal. It even eats people. Crocodiles carry out hundreds of attacks on humans each year, many of them fatal.

Crocodiles are ambush predators. They may lie in wait for hours before prey comes near. Then they lunge.

Under Threat

The gharial is a critically endangered crocodilian that lives in Asia. There are only around 200 left in the wild. In the past these reptiles were hunted for their skins. Today, many of their river habitats have been dammed. The sand banks where gharials nest are being used by farmers to graze cattle.

The gharial's long, thin snout is too small and weak to take large prey. It has sharp, thin teeth for catching fish.

AMERICAN ALLIGATOR

ALLIGATOR MISSISSIPPIENSIS
"MISSISSIPPI LIZARD"

Habitat: Lakes, swamps; southern USA
Length: Male 3.4 m (11.2 ft); female 2.6 m (8.5 ft)
Weight: Male 270 kg (595 lb); female 120 kg (265 lb)
Diet: Fish, birds, turtles, mammals
Lifespan: Up to 50 years
Wild population: 5 million; Least Concern

The alligator has about 80 teeth. When they wear out or break, new ones grow. Over its life an alligator might have 3,000 teeth.

The alligator's snout is wide, rounded, and black. A crocodile's is different—it is narrow, pointed, and olive-green.

The alligator's underside has smooth scales, but its back is covered with bony plates. These protect the alligator and help to disguise it as a floating log.

Fish

More than half of vertebrates are fish. These cold-blooded animals live in salt or fresh water, have tails and body fins, breathe through gills, and usually have scales. There are around 28,000 species, from the 12.65-m (41.5-ft) whale shark to a tiny swamp carp that measures just 8 mm (0.3 in).

Staying Safe

Many species limit the risk of being eaten by larger fish by sticking together in schools for safety. Other fish have amazing camouflage to avoid being seen. Speed and swimming prowess save the lives of some fish. Others have defensive spines, scales, or toxins.

The parrotfish is named for its beak-like mouth, designed for biting chunks of coral off the reef.

The puffer fish transforms itself if an enemy appears. It takes in enough water to double in size. The fish is suddenly ball-shaped, and covered with poison-tipped spines.

Extraordinary Eels

Eels look more like snakes than fish. Long and thin, they move by wriggling. Eels are found in the sea and fresh water and most don't have scales. Some species can even move on land. Eels usually spend the day hiding in rocky crevices and come out at night to hunt.

The giant moray eel is a predator that lives on coral reefs. It can grow as long as 3 m (9.8 ft).

At night, the parrotfish covers its body with slimy mucus. This hides its scent from nocturnal hunters.

The fish's gills are behind the cheek flap. They take oxygen from the water and produce waste carbon dioxide.

Moving the tail fin from side to side generates thrust. It propels the fish forward in the water.

STOPLIGHT PARROTFISH

SPARISOMA VIRIDE
"GOLDEN-HEADED GREEN FISH"

Habitat: Coral reefs; W Atlantic
Length: Male 50 cm (1.6 ft); female 30 cm (1 ft)
Weight: Male 1.6 kg (3.5 lb); female 1.4 kg (3.1 lb)
Diet: Coral polyps, algae
Lifespan: Up to 30 years
Wild population: Unknown; Least Concern

Sharks

Sharks are fish with skeletons made of tough, flexible cartilage instead of bone. They first appeared 220 million years before the dinosaurs. Today there are more than 500 species. Sharks have a reputation as fierce predators, but most species are harmless and shark attacks are rare.

All Shapes and Sizes

Most sharks— including the great white, tiger, blue, bull, mako, and reef sharks —have a sleek, streamlined body. Others are very different shapes. In deep waters, the frilled shark is long and eel-like, while the goblin shark is named for its unusual nose. The flattened bodies of angel sharks and wobbegongs suit life on the seabed.

The skin is as rough as sandpaper. It is covered with grooved, tooth-shaped scales that direct the flow of water over the shark's body and reduce drag.

The great white has an excellent sense of taste. It can detect a few drops of blood in the water from 5 km (3 miles) away.

The shark has rows of sharp, triangular teeth up to 7.5 cm (3 in) long. As old ones are lost, new teeth move forward to take their place.

There are ten species of hammerhead. These sharks have a T-shaped head with eyes far apart, which gives them a wide field of vision.

A torpedo-shaped body, pointed at each end, cuts down water resistance. The shark swims at 40 km/h (25 mph).

Filter-Feeders

The three largest shark species—the whale shark, basking shark, and megamouth—do not hunt large prey. They take in water through their enormous, gaping mouth, and then force it out again through their gills. Their filter pads capture microscopic plants and animals from the water.

A whale shark's mouth is 1.5 m (4.9 ft) wide. It contains more than 300 rows of tiny teeth and ten filter pads for sieving plankton from seawater.

GREAT WHITE SHARK

CARCHARODON CARCHARIAS
"POINTED TOOTH"

Habitat: Oceans worldwide except the poles
Length: Male 4 m (13.1 ft); female 4.5m (14.8 ft)
Weight: Male 800 kg (1,764 lb); female 1,000 kg (2,205 lb)
Diet: Fish incl. sharks, turtles, marine mammals
Lifespan: Up to 70 years
Wild population: Unknown; Vulnerable

Creepy-crawlies

Creepy-crawlies are small invertebrates. They include an estimated 30 million insect species, as well as arachnids, such as spiders and scorpions, millipedes and centipedes, and worms. Some mollusks and crustaceans also count as creepy-crawlies.

The woodlouse belongs to the same family as crabs and lobsters. It is a crustacean.

Count the Legs!

The word "insect" means "cut into pieces," and an adult insect always has three parts to its body—head, thorax, and abdomen. It also always has six legs in its adult form. A creepy-crawly with more or less than six legs is not an insect. Insects often have wings, but not always.

PRAYING MANTIS

MANTIS RELIGIOSA

Habitat: Fields, woods, grasslands; S Asia, S Europe, N America, Australia
Length: Male 6 cm (2.4 in); female 7.5 cm (3 in)
Weight: Male 2.5 g (0.09 oz); female 3 g (0.11 oz)
Diet: Insects, mantids, other invertebrates
Lifespan: Up to 9 months
Wild population: Unknown; Least Concern

The praying mantis shoots out its front legs to grasp insect prey, such as grasshoppers and crickets.

Recycling Machines

Creepy-crawlies that eat dead plants and animals are known as detritivores. Earthworms, millipedes, slugs, and woodlice are all detritivores. They do a useful job in the food chain because they reuse nutrients, so these do not go to waste.

The shocking pink dragon millipede eats rotting leaves. It protects itself from predators by producing cyanide, a deadly poison.

The long body can be green, yellow, brown, or even black. It has two pairs of wings. Females cannot fly with their wings, but males can.

43

Spiders and Scorpions

Along with mites and ticks, scorpions and spiders are arachnids. There are at least 45,700 species of spider and 1,750 scorpions. They are eight-legged predators with no antennae or wings. All scorpions and most spiders have venom, but few are fatal to humans.

Super Spiders

All spiders spin silk, but not all build webs. From spiral orbs to tubes and funnels, spider webs are used to trap prey. Other spiders have different hunting methods. The trapdoor spider ambushes prey from a hidden lair, while the huntsman gives chase. Spiders range in size from a pinhead-sized orbweb to the massive goliath tarantula.

A crab spider has eight eyes to see in all directions. It lies in wait, perfectly disguised, ready to ambush insect visitors to the flower.

The leg-like pedipalps on either side of the jaws crush and tear up food.

The two front walking legs are also used to grasp bees, flies, and other prey.

The world's biggest spider, the goliath tarantula, can weigh 175 g (6.2 oz). It hunts mice, lizards, and small birds.

There are more than 2,000 species of crab spider. Many match the flowers where they hunt for insect prey each day.

Sting in the Tail

While spiders inject venom with their fangs, the scorpion produces venom from a stinger at the end of its curving tail. It stings to protect itself from predators. It can also stun struggling prey, but usually it saves its venom and kills prey with its powerful pincers.

Scorpions are tough survivors, found in many harsh habitats. This yellow fattail scorpion lives in deserts in North Africa and the Middle East.

CRAB SPIDER

THOMISUS ONUSTUS

Habitat: Moors, deserts, grasslands; Europe, Asia, Africa
Length: Male 4 mm (0.16 in); female 7 mm (0.28 in)
Weight: Male 2.5 g (0.09 oz); female 3 g (0.11 oz)
Diet: Small invertebrates
Lifespan: Up to 4 months
Wild population: Unknown

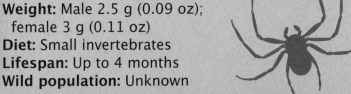

Bees

Worldwide, excluding Antarctica, there are about 20,000 bee species. Most live alone, but honeybees and bumblebees form large colonies, made up of a queen bee, hundreds of drones, and thousands of workers. The drones mate with the queen. The workers guard the nest, collect pollen and nectar, and care for young.

Breaking Away

When a bee colony becomes too large, the queen bee lays eggs that will develop into queens instead of worker bees. She leaves the nest with a large group of workers. The swarm flies to a suitable site to start a new colony. When they get there, the queen starts laying eggs already fertilized by the drones.

A swarm can contain hundreds or even thousands of honeybees.

Each leg is split into segments, so it is very flexible.

The bee has a pair of jointed antennae. They can touch, smell, taste, and pick up vibrations.

The bumblebee has two pairs of wings. They beat up and down so quickly that they make a buzzing noise.

GARDEN BUMBLEBEE

BOMBUS HORTORUM
"PLANT BUZZER"

Habitat: Grasslands, farmland; Europe, Asia, New Zealand
Length: 1.5 cm (0.6 in); queen 2 cm (0.8 in)
Weight: 2.5 g (0.09 oz); queen 4 g (0.14 oz)
Diet: Nectar, pollen
Lifespan: Up to 2 weeks; queen up to 1 year
Wild population: Unknown; Least Concern

46

Many plants need bees to pollinate them so that they can produce fruit.

Female bumblebees can sting. Their sting is not barbed like a honeybee's, so it can be reused many times.

Finding Food

Honeybees carry nectar and pollen back to the hive. They mix nectar with saliva to make honey to feed the young. When bees find a good source of nectar, they tell the other workers where it is with an elaborate, waggling dance.

The hairy body picks up grains of pollen, which rub off on the next flower the bee visits. This is called pollination.

Bees store honey in hexagonal cells, which they build from beeswax. The cells also house eggs and larvae.

Glossary

AMBUSH PREDATOR
A hunting animal that waits in one place for prey to come close rather than hunting by speed or strength.

ANTENNA (pl: ANTENNAE)
One of a pair of sensory feelers on an invertebrate's head.

BALEEN
A flexible keratin plate inside the mouth of some whales, which filters plankton from the water.

CARNIVORE
An animal that eats meat.

CARRION
A dead animal's decaying body.

CARTILAGE
A lightweight, flexible material that makes up the skeleton of some animals, such as sharks.

CRUSTACEAN
An arthropod with two-part legs and a hard shell.

EVOLVE
To change from one species to another over millions of years, by passing on particular characteristics from one generation to the next.

EXTINCT
Describes an animal that has died out forever.

FERTILIZED
Describes a female cell that has combined with a male cell and can develop into a new living thing.

FOOD CHAIN
A series of animals, each of which depends on the next for food.

GRAZER
An animal that eats grass.

HABITAT
An animal's natural environment.

HERBIVORE
An animal that eats plants.

HIBERNATE
To slow the body right down in winter in a kind of sleep.

INVERTEBRATE
An animal that has no backbone.

KRILL
A small, shrimp-like crustacean that is part of plankton.

MAMMAL
A warm-blooded vertebrate that has hair or fur and feeds its young on mother's milk.

MIGRATION
A regular journey that an animal makes at the same time each year, for example to feed or breed.

PINCER
A claw that opens and closes.

POLLUTION
Damage to the environment from poisons and garbage produced by humans.

PREDATOR
An animal that hunts and eats other animals.

PREY
An animal that is hunted and eaten by other animals for food.

RAIN FOREST
A thick, usually evergreen forest, often tropical, that receives more than 254 cm (100 in) of rain a year.

SPECIES
One particular type of living thing. Members of the same species often look similar and produce fertile offspring together.

TERRITORY
The area that an animal defends against other animals, usually of the same species.

TUNDRA
Flat, treeless plains within the Arctic circle, where the ground is permanently frozen.

VENOM
A chemical that is injected into another animal to paralyze or kill.

VERTEBRATE
An animal that has a backbone.

WINGSPAN
The width of a flying animal's outstretched wings, from wing tip to wing tip.